*The
Pilgrimage
of*
FATHERHOOD

A Poetry Chapbook by
R. Michael Spangler

Copyright 2020 by R. Michael Spangler
All rights reserved

No part of this book may be reproduced, stored in a retrieval system, or transmitted in any form or by any means, electronic, mechanical, photocopying, recording, or otherwise, without the prior written permission of the author.

ISBN 978-1-7360805-0-4

Scripture quotations are from the ESV® Bible (The Holy Bible, English Standard Version®), copyright © 2001 by Crossway, a publishing ministry of Good News Publishers. Used by permission. All rights reserved.

Cover photo by Andy Stratton

https://rmspangler.com/

To my children, who cheekily tell me that I'm the second best dad in the world (after God). That's exactly what I want to be for them.

Preface

I am the father of four amazing children. Almost nothing has brought me as much joy as being a dad. That said, nothing has humbled me like being a dad either.

Depending on who I talk to, I get either affirming head nods or a confused head turn when I share my struggles with fatherhood. Every person has a unique story and every household has a unique dynamic. There is no cookie-cutter formula for the pilgrimage of fatherhood.

I grew up lacking a consistent father figure in my life but I never realized its effect on me until I became a father myself. Since I did not have the fatherly presence I needed, I thought that if I simply showed up for my kids, I would succeed. I thought, *I'm going to be the dad who's there for them at every turn, every tear, every joy. I'm going to right this ship.* And yet, scars and sin from deep within me began to surface—anger, depression, breakdowns, unrealistic expectations, and feelings of past abandonment all surfaced from what seemed like nowhere.

Fatherhood is a transformative journey, and it is not easy. There are pitfalls to the left and to the right. Danger from behind and obstacles ahead. If we are going to succeed, we cannot run on the fumes of self-reliance or put demands on our children that they cannot bear. From where does our help come?

I hope to be a gentle guide on this journey, because I am not an exemplary model. Fellow pilgrim, I am in this caravan with you.

How good it is that we a heavenly Father who will never leave nor forsake us. I cannot emphasize enough the need for receiving God's means of grace: humbly coming before him through scripture reading and prayer; clinging, like a helpless beggar, to his promises (Isa 41:10, 49:15; Lam 3:21–23; Rom 8:32; 2 Cor 4:17–18; Phil 4:19, 12–13; seriously, look these up); and seeking help from older men (thank you, Bud Burk).

Counseling, in particular, has given me better understanding and deeper insight. The book of Proverbs says, "The purpose in a man's heart is like deep water, but a man of understanding will draw it out" (Prov 20:5). One unexpected thing I learned about myself from therapy was the importance of poetry. Poetry supplies language for the heart. And my hope is that this language will be a help to you—a means of grace for your pilgrimage. You are not alone in the joys or the struggles.

May the God of hope fill you with all joy and peace in believing, so that by the power of the Holy Spirit you may abound in hope (Rom 15:13).

Rob Spangler, 2020

Onward In Life's Armada

I have one little ship in life's armada.
It's not a perfect vessel, but it's mine for now.

There are times when I trail behind the big ships, seeking guidance. Other times I'm in the lead, helping newer captains.

Too often, I've fallen asleep or into my pride. But my first mate bails me out. We'd still be in the harbor without her. There's a lot of love between my shipmates, though mutinous screams are heard from time to time. This is our ship, and I've been trusted to lead it.

The empty horizon lets me know that we're off course, again. The sun slips under the blanket of the sea. All seems lost. It's the dark of night. The King's ship pulls away to rescue us. He reminds me of His map. By dawn, we're on track once again.

Each storm has made me question this seafaring vessel. Or, at least my job sailing it. It has been submerged, nearly shipwrecked. But lo, it comes up, paradoxically stronger than when it swam in the fair-weather.

So, onward we sail through this dark sea.
We're on our journey home to a place we've never seen.
His map never fails and my King is with me.

So, onward we sail.

May Poem

On the eleventh day of May
A cry echoed the halls
Of Mercy Hospital.
Two cries, really.
Mom's, because it was finally over.
Mine, because it had just begun.

I left the safe darkness of the womb
For the sterile darkness of the world.
Its cold shot through my tiny frame,
As frantic nurses persuaded Dad to
Snip the tether to my old world.

There's no going back now, just
Stumbling through the dark, for eighteen years.
Pressing on with the memory of warmth,
Desperately looking for a light switch.

Only to find that I must be born,
again.

The Answers We Hear

Child, you can't have purpose yet.
You'll find it when you go to school.

Young man, you're tired of impressing them?
It will be better at the university.

Friend, the enjoyment was short-lived?
Get married and have kids.

Man, it's difficult you say?
Retirement is where you'll find rest.

Sir, not well today?
There'll be peace when you die.

Trust me.
Have I ever steered you wrong?

I Love To Hear You Cry

For my son, Judah

I love to hear you cry

Not because it sounds so shrill
Nor the strength of your will

Not because of your fear
Nor even your messy rear

It's not the pain you feel
When you haven't had a meal

But when life's cord tied its knot—
You and death fought

I love to hear you cry
Because we almost did not

Rocking This Crying Baby

As I sit here, rocking this crying baby
I'm reminded of all the pressing
emails yet to be written and replied to.
A pile of dishes with microwaved
cheese stains. I'm supposed to be
maximizing my productivity, ten times-ing
my income, and implementing ten incredible
new life hacks this very moment.

These anxious thoughts sink me deep
into this rocking chair, making me wonder.
What if success is the monotonous,
back-and-forth creaking of an old chair?
And I'm exactly where I should be.
Defiantly rocking this crying baby,
without another care in the world.

Dad's Shadow

Umbra

I can't escape Dad's shadow
It follows me everywhere I…
Go! I wanted to be better
To straighten this crooked road

Penumbra

But I can't escape your shadow
Now my son is trapped in
mine. Flesh and heart have failed
I can't see the finish line

Antumbra

So I hide myself in God
To You, darkness is day-
light. You won't leave nor forsake
You're the morning to this night

Lux

Reveal what lies beneath
Mortify sin's whole not in
part. On the cross, it's done
You save my failing heart

The Builder Levels Me

I'm a firefly boasting of his tail to the sun.
Better off is a child crying for milk.

I was building a castle to the highest clouds.
It was made of my finest sand.

And you leveled it like
a crashing wave.
And me with
Your plow.

Over and over.
Again and again.
Through and through.
Left in desolation's wake.

Was it because your anger grew?
Or, could it be your mercy anew?

You said you're preparing a home for me,
A home with many rooms.
I'll let go of pride to let you be,
The master-builder of what I can't see.

I long for your embrace.
To feel your gentle, gritty hands.
Not as Thomas, for proof.
But as a child, for comfort.

What is, is not what ought and a
Plentiful redemption is coming.

The groaning land will be fruitful again.
Weary people will have rest again.
Wary people will be secure again.

My hope is in the Lord.
My hope is in the Lord.

Dad's Ashes

I remember brother's call that morning,
Then seeing you motionless on the bed.
Your wife, confused and frantic in mourning.
Your eyes, at rest in the back of your head.

I choked speechless bursts at your eulogy,
Knowing I had lost what was never mine,
Wishing for just one more ride, you and me,
Hand on your knee—comfort you one more time.

But it's to ashes you have now returned.
The wind blows, as grass you westwardly fade.
We watch to see what He'll make from what's burned.
God's furnace makes gold from little green blades.

It's ashes for now, glory for later.
We look upon things unseen, yet greater.

Solid Rock

I've seen mighty men fall
Men stronger than you
Die.

If the ground is shaky
The house will
Fall.

But I've seen dead men walk
Men weaker than you
Live.

The house built
On solid rock
Stands.

Men Watch Sports

Men watch sports.
Strong men.
Men with beards.
And beers.
And four-letter words.

I like books.
And poetry.
And four-syllable words.
An ef-fem-i-nate
de-tes-ta-tion to men.

But have you ever read
David's Psalms?

Handy Man

I remember when I fixed
The kitchen sink
It was time to be a man

So I muscled up
Turned the wrench
And got it done

Nobody taught me how to fix
A kitchen sink
That's probably why it broke

Again, and a time after
Until we called
The handyman

I've never been a handy man
My fingers remain softened by
This keyboard

What is a man, anyway?
Nobody had time
To show me

So I muscle up
Turn the wrench
And try again

But the sinks still leak

Contra Mundum

Whispers echo in silent room
Walls alone to drink their sound
Like a tomb robbed and bare
Possessions snatched by darkest plot

The greedy weapon used to strike
Only reveals treasure beneath
Not in a safe or stretched from reach
But living there in quiet heart

Abiding treasure which remains
As shielded by the Savior's might
Treasure that topples all earth's weight
Great joy and forever delight

Rich young man, one thing you lack
Though the world you seem to have
Rich young man, give all you own
Then you shall lack none but lack

Pro Mundum

Air filled with songs of creation
Laughter compiled its sweet refrain

Cup of coffee with rising steam
Reflects pleasures above, received

Pops of air from crackling wood
Soaking red warmth from coals beneath

Snuggled in beds of joyous rest
A story fills the quiet night

Bright stars replace the fading sky
Hidden promises now revealed

Lungs make ready for the valley
As this mountain air is breathed

Not Like This

After my stepfather's suicide

Can you forgive a man
If he's no longer here?

Can you apologize
If he'll never hear?

Every little sheep needs a shepherd
But to me you were a hired hand
I ran from you at every word
I ignored your every command

Your lips bore the mark of your teeth
Your stare bore a mark in my mind
I just wanted you to be gone
To leave us all behind

But not like this
Not at all like this
As harsh as you were to me
I also have a list

The lies that I told
You exposed in the light
The call that I made
To the police that night

The things I said
To prod my dad's fight

But I never said I'm sorry
I never made it right

Now I'm left in the silence
And though I'm not the same
You never got to see
The man that I became

Though you're not here
I forgive you

Though you can't hear
I'm so sorry

Rest, Little Restless One

For my son, Ezra

Rest, little restless one
It's been a stormy day
We've felt the waves of life
But now it's time to say

Rest, little restless one
Daddy doesn't want to fight
We don't need a bed or pillows
Daddy's arm is just right

You're determined, little restless one
A wild wind that propels
Today your strength digs holes
Tomorrow it'll dig wells

Rest, little restless one
We'll end hard days like this
A smile in your eyes
And on your cheek a kiss

I love you, my son
Now rest, little restless one

I Didn't Expect To Find You There

The day was average;
my task was ordinary.
I didn't expect to find you there.

The scent of Polo Green
brought you
right next to me.

The gentleness of your greeting,
the kindness of your eyes,
the sandy feel of your hard-working hands.

Our past friction has melted away,
the fondness has grown fonder,
our reconciliation has become more precious.

I didn't expect to find you there.
I even looked for you, Dad,
but I didn't see you.

I still have to wait.

Sehnsucht Der Tochter (Daughter's Longing)

For my daughter, Elliana

Little one, you're always longing
Crying out, "I want to go home"
Waiting is only prolonging
The feeling that you're all alone

Little one, "Home is where you are"
But, that's not entirely true
You're aching for a home that's far
Where everything'll be made new

This world won't satisfy that need
You were made for somewhere better
A place with no tears, death, nor greed
A place we can be together

Yet they're not that place's true prize
They're just some of its many charms
It's the light of Jesus's eyes
When he brings you into his arms

But don't pack up now, little one
It's not yet time for us to leave
The Kingdom shines here, like the sun
For the little ones to receive

A Secret For My Kids

I have a secret.
Well, I have a few secrets.
But this secret, you already
know about.

It's the secret seen
in my eyes
when they get shiny
after I yell at you.

When you're scared,
I'm scared of failing you.
When you're scared,
I'm scared of ruining you.

I was supposed to be different—
the one to right this ship.
And sometimes I turn the wheel
so hard, my fingers bleed.

Or, sometimes I'm
so weak, I break.
Then I wonder if God can sail me
home and give you someone stronger.

And yet, he keeps giving you,
me. And he keeps giving me,
you. He keeps giving us
new mercies, every morning.

Why do I tell you this secret?
Because nobody told me theirs.
And my failure is mine.
And there's hope for you.

Hope in a heavenly Father
who will never leave you,
nor forsake you. He will not
forget you, nor lose you.

And that Father is going to
help this father never
leave you, nor forsake you.
Never forget you, nor lose you.

And that, is a secret worth sharing.

My Greatest Art

The greatest art that comes from me
Won't be a poem or PhD
I'm often pulled by vanity
A slave to what others just might see

I see abundance of work undone
Rather than playing with my son
I ache for days of solitude
Neglecting God's true bread for food

I show you just how great I am
With my personal online hologram
The joy it promises by likes and loves
Is fleeting pleasure, not from above

It blows away with the wind
Yet there I go, I try again
Give me food that satisfies
Not these transient, little lies

Oh Spirit, come and sanctify
Don't waste these longing tears I cry
The greatest art that comes from me
Is all this life I give to thee

My First Arrow

For my son, Micah

You are the first arrow of my quiver,
But I am afraid to pull back the bow.
It feels safer in the woods upriver,

For my target lies beyond a vile foe.
Past a world that promises all you need,
Where human arrows always veer too low.

I wish I could send you past with such speed
That you'd surpass vanity and greed, yet
It's not by my strength that you will succeed.

Christ was the one who poured his blood and sweat.
Keeping the law and yet, a lamb before
Shearers, gave himself as price for our debt.

So, I pull the bow as a man of war,
Trusting the King with my precious arrow.
Shine bright as you go. He will make you soar.

Die Like A Leaf

I want to die
Like a leaf in autumn.
To go out in a blaze
Of brilliant colors,
Reflecting the fire
Of a life well-lived.
Like Elijah, who was
Enveloped in a whirlwind.
Or Moses, whose
Face shone the glory
Of God in his old age.

Instead, I'll probably
Be more like that old
Burnt-looking, crinkled
Leaf that just wouldn't
Surrender the fight.
I'll hang on long past
My time, spinning to make
Up for the lack of
Fire from yesteryears.
I'll long for home
But grapple with fears.

Finally, the last breeze
Will come to take me away.
My children will try
And catch me on the

Way down, with
Experimental treatments
Or an all-organic diet.
But I'll evade their
Grasp and crash
To the ground,
Where all the leaves go.

But when the Gardener
Tenderly picks me up,
I'll finally be a blaze
Of brilliant colors.
Brighter than
My drab imagination
Could have conjured.

More poems and writings @
https://rmspangler.com/

www.ingramcontent.com/pod-product-compliance
Lightning Source LLC
Chambersburg PA
CBHW031509040426
42444CB00007B/1269